Picking up the Pieces

Cherokee Mcalpine

Picking up the Pieces

First Edition: 2022

ISBN: 9781524318024
ISBN eBook: 9781524328092

© of the text:
  Cherokee Mcalpine

© Layout, design and production of this edition: 2022
EBL

All rights reserved. No part of this publication may be reproduced, distributed, or transmitted in any form or by any means, including photocopying, recording, or other electronic or mechanical methods, without the prior written permission of the Publisher.

Dedicated to my Grandpa Art, who influenced my love for reading, my siblings Natasha (Angel) and Eugene (Geno), who loved me unconditionally, and my foster parents Kay and Jason, and Martha (Marty) and Gareth (Gary) for showing me what it means to be loved and to love.

Table of Contents

Away 13
Dreams 14
Need 15
They Say 16
I 17
I Cry 18
I Try 19
After Death 20
Me:them 21
My Pain 22
Difference 23
Life at Home 24
Blood From the Soul 25
What Do We Do? 26
Voices of Fear 27
Touch 29
Life 30
If You 31
When You 32

Take a Chance	33
Used to	34
I Resented You	35
I Never Knew	36
16 Scars	37
Newtown Tragedy	38
When	40
When I Was	41
Why	42
I Want to be	43
Strong	44
My Wings	45
Secret Angel	46
Path to my Past	47
Fear of Death	48
You Said	49
Loss	50
You'd Never Know	51
Fate	52
Life	53
Music	54
Run	55
Love	56
Fight	57

Go	58
Tears	59
Never	60
You'll Never Know	61
Do You?	62
Broken	64
You Need to Know	66
Questions For You	68
My Heart	70
Tried to Let it Go	72
Looking	73
The End	86
One Minus One	87
Again	88
Light of Love	90
Addiction	93
Monster	95
Death	96
Anger Red	97
Love to Death	98
Tear It Apart	99
That's When You Know	100
Depression	102
The Hallway	103

Take a Pill	106
Thing Called Anxiety	107
Saying Goodbye	109
His Obsession	110
Five Monsters	111
False Good-Luck Charm	112
The Final Ado	113
The Cliff's Edge	114
You and I	119
'Till Death Do Us Part	121
Past, Present, Future	123
Dear Mental Illness	128
The Journey	130
Conquered	132
Hold my Heart	134
Meant to Be	135
Pressure	137
Eternal Slumber	138
The Final Battle	139

I feel like an animal set free then put back in the cage. I'm trapped. I'm starving for a friend. I'm lost. I miss my freedom. People keep throwing me hope like it's food and take it away. They promise to help let me lose and push me further into my cage. I'm frightened to death. I'm dying. I'm failing, I can't get through the gate. I'm trapped in my mind. I can't get out. Every time I'm close to the key, someone takes it.

Time stands still. I'm frozen in place, I can't move. I'm stranded on an island. I'm in-caged in a cage. I'm trapped in ice. I can't escape. No one can reach me. I'm failing, I'm dying. I'm lost. I'm stranded on a cliff trying to decide whether to jump or not. If I jump, I'm free of all the pain and if I don't I can well... have temporary friends, temporary happiness. I'm a failure. I'm dying in undeciding decision.

AWAY

Please, don't leave me alone
      Keep me with you
      Don't say goodbye
      Stay with me
Stop, don't hurt me anymore
      Stay away from me
      Don't touch me
      Leave me be
Please, keep me by your side
      Don't let me go
      Hold on to me
      Never release me
Stop, don't hold onto me
      Don't grab my hand
      Keep away
      Let me be.

DREAMS

If you want to touch the stars
Then put your dreams to that limit
If you want to walk on the moon
Then fly through outer space
If you want to soar with the birds
Then let your wings become real
If you want to run like the river
Then let your tears flow

NEED

When you want the sun
I'll try and get it
When you fall down
I'll help you up
When you are sad
I'll give you a tissue
When you feel helpless
I'll give you a helping hand
When you have a broken heart
I'll give you my heart
When you need support
I'll give you my help
When you are crying
I'll give you my shoulder to cry on

THEY SAY

They say it's okay to cry
So I cry
They say it's brave to speak out
So I speak out
They say I should be assertive
So I'm assertive
They say it's okay to feel
So I feel

I

I close my eyes
And the pain fades away
I breathe deeply
And my lungs feel better
I slow down
And my heart seems stronger
I start to love
And my heart doesn't seem so broken
I take chances
And I seem to get closer to success
I start to change
And I can see better
I start talking
And the pressure lessens

I CRY

When I fail
I cry
When I'm upset
I cry
When I'm worried
I cry
When I'm depressed
I cry
When I'm frustrated
I cry
When I'm yelled at
I cry
When someone's mad at me
I cry

I TRY

I try to sustain my unfailing tears
But I cry a river
I try to control the pain
But I grow weaker
I try to speak up for myself
But my voice fails to work

AFTER DEATH

I see the blood
Whose is it?
I see my body
I'm dead
I wonder what happened?
I killed myself
I wonder why?
I hated life
Family and friends come
They're strangers
Everyone weeps for me
They didn't know me
People are all in tears
It can't bring me back
Everyone asks why and what I have to say
I'm sorry, I was in pain
Everyone buries me and prays
I leave

ME:THEM

I look around: It's dark
I try to breathe: I choke
I cry out: no one hears
I pass on: no one notices
I give up: others just give in
I cry: no one seems to care
I try to look happy: everyone is satisfied
I think about the pain: others get mad
I give up on life: now people care
I'm dead: people say they miss me

MY PAIN

It's in my eyes
It's my tears
My heart
It's in my arms
It's my life
I struggle to breath
And cling to my source of light
But I'm going blind
I won't be able to see soon
I'll live in darkness
I start to die
I'm falling through air
Help me! I cry

DIFFERENCE

Take a look at me
Do you see the difference?
Is it my hair?
My eyes?
My lips?
My nose?
My height?
My weight?
My legs?
My arms?
Do you see the difference?

LIFE AT HOME

When my pain was bad and my cage was taking me from sane
I tried to end it all
But my preventer prevented me my pain
I yelled and cried
About it all
That why I always tried
My life wasn't perfect of right
So I never failed to notice
All your mighty might
Never did they care
Or see the bruises
My life was never fair
I tired and tired
To dry my tears
But I just cried and cried
I tried and tried
But always lost
It felt like sin
Of all I lost
My freedom
Was my biggest cost

BLOOD FROM THE SOUL

The touch so light, the feeling so bright
The tear is a wonderful, magical thing
The wonder it makes me feel when I see them cry
Tear after tear
Weep after weep
Sob after sob
The blood of the soul is sinless

WHAT DO WE DO?

What do you do when the worst is coming?
When life is failing to notice you and you're heading down the wrong path?
What do you do?
Ange is an infectious disease
No one understands my life
What do I do?
Life is like an angelic moment
A once in a blue moon
One breath is like the world is in your hands
What can I do?
We can't always be right can we?
I know my life is special
We're all for a purpose

VOICES OF FEAR

How do you know when to stop worrying?
When is life ever fair?
My body cries out in protest
My mind say stop
My gut say it's no use
My heart says it's ok, you can do it
I shake with fear, of all the doubt
I try to shake away the voices
They say stop
You're not worth it
You're dumb
You can't do it
You life is as useless as garbage
So many different voices shout at me, saying different things
I'm confused
I feel like I'm falling through nothingness
Why is life so difficult?

Why is it so hard to make friends and keep them? Why is it hard to build up the courage to sprout up a conversation?

Life is like a puzzle with all different sizes of puzzle pieces

TOUCH

The touch hurts
It's painful
We can't handle it
Our life is worthless
We don't mean a thing
We're sinful
We bleed from the touches
We cry from the pain
We die in vain
Every scream is impossible
We can't escape
We're trapped
We're scared for life
Our heart is broken
Do you still not know?
Is it hard to see?
The marks upon her skin
She's dying
Failing to be loved
It hurts

LIFE

It's all over
I can't go on any longer
Can't fake it
Can't take it
I'm failing to live
I'm falling down
My breath is stopping
I can't live any longer with this pain
But everything may fall and get back up
But everything may someday be gone
And we'll live to watch the moon
And everyone gets back up on their feet

IF YOU

If you look closely
You'll see my tears
If you watch intentionally
You'll notice I'm sad
If you cut deeply
You'll see a broken heart
If you say it lovingly
You may see that I believe it

WHEN YOU

When you hurt me
You hurt me bad
When you left
You left me broken
When you neglected me
You neglected me it all
When you rejected me
You rejected me in pain
When you ignored me
You ignored my tears
When you gave me up
You gave me up to the unknown

TAKE A CHANCE

Take a chance
And let it go
Take a chance
And be the best
Take a chance
And say you love me
Take a chance
And make a change
Take a chance
And let your wings soar

USED TO

I used to hit you
But now I am sorry
You used to cry to me
And I ignored you
I used to say "I hate you"
And I really meant it
You used to get on my nerves
And I yelled at you
I used to deny it
But now I face the truth
I used to avoid my feelings
But now I face everything

I RESENTED YOU

I resented you because
You were the perfect little angel
I resented you because
You weren't hurt as much as me
I resented you because
You cared about me and what I did
I resented you because
You never fought back
I resented you because
You got things I didn't
I resented you and I still do

I NEVER KNEW

I never knew I'd miss it
But now it's gone
I never knew I'd say it
But I did
I never knew I'd feel it
But now it's overwhelming
I never knew I'd leave it
But I've moved
I never knew I'd discover it
But now I have

16 SCARS

I'd tried and failed and failed again
To be the daughter they wanted
We wanted to be loved but
Each day they hated us more
One day when it was 6-8-9
We did our bidding wrong
They took the cord
So hot, fierce, and angry
He beat us down
With cuts and blood
16's my number
Half was my pain
8 was my punishment
Theirs 6 and 9
Yell as I might
No one heard a thing
16's my number
16 are my scars

NEWTOWN TRAGEDY

(Poem about the Sandy Hook Elementary Shooting Dec 14th, 2012)
Tears
There's too many
Our spirits fade with each last breath
26 deaths
Many more tears
There's too much pain
Life is stopping
They feel like they are suffocating
Unopened gifts
Undone hopes
Lost dreams
Will life ever be the same
They can't move on
20 young lives taken in a single blast
Why?
The noise deafens them
Tragedy has struck
Why?
No one knows

God bless the young and old
Help us they cry
My baby's dead
We can't go on
Tears
We cry on and on
Then we say goodbye

WHEN

When we were together
Your pain was forever
When we were alone
I had a mean tone
When we were enemies
We were frenemies
When you were my sister
I was bitter

WHEN I WAS

When I was glad
You were glad
When I was mad
You were mad
When I was sad
You were sad
When I was depressed
You were depressed
When I was angry
You were angry
When I was a victim
You were a victim
When I was the abused
You were the abused
When I was the abuser
You were the abused

WHY

Why, in life, do people love to hurt you?
lie to you and set you up?
Why are people so mean?
Why do they call you names?
Or hurt you with words?
Why or why?

I WANT TO BE

12 years gone and past, it flew by so fast
I never thought I'd make it through
Yet here I am on the other side
I tried to hide, tried to find my way through life
When I thought I should die, I said
Let's prove them wrong, let's make they see
I can be anything I want to be
Just 'cause I'm on the bottom, doesn't mean
I can't get to the top, I can win
'Cause I can be anything I want to be

STRONG

She was beaten down and disrespected, but she
Got back up and never gave in
When they told her she's never make it, she got
Up and proved them wrong
She shed blood and tears in secrecy, but she
Stopped and moved on
When she was hit and pulled down, she prayed
And took a breath

MY WINGS

My wings are colored and beaten
They are red from the anger I've shed
They are black from my impure past
They are gray from all my inner thoughts
They are sprained from flying from myself
They are fractured from hitting my blockades
They are broken from falling to the ground
I' an angel that fell and got back up
I've got a dark past and it's made me beautiful
My wings are my story of pain and hope

SECRET ANGEL

I soared high above everyone but only to hide my wings
I was once pure white, but some feathers have darkened
I tried to cover up my colors but people noticed
I think I'm an ugly one but they think it's beautiful
I have white wings but dark colors are hidden
Yes, I'm a bright angel with a dark past

PATH TO MY PAST

My eyes are the key
My heart the door
My soul the treasure
My mind the warrior
Look into my eyes and see my past, there's the key
Show you care and truly love me, the door is open
Make a difference in my life, you have the treasure
Fight beside me and the warrior becomes your friend
Hurt me and all of me, my eyes, heart, soul, and mind
Will shut you out and fight you no matter what

FEAR OF DEATH

They come and go, weaving in and out
We can't predict our futures
The doom seems inevitable
The light is fading into the distance
The noises can't be heard
Our plea to be spared is lost in the wind

YOU SAID

You said you loved me
Yet you hit me
You said I could trust you
Yet you distanced yourself
You said I'd never get hurt
Yet you proved yourself wrong

LOSS

The feeling is lost in the wind
I can't see or hear what it says
I'm numb
I can't feel the pain anymore
I'm too worn out to understand
I've run so dry I'm thirsty for it
I don't know how to get it back
How to fill myself with the pain I crave
I can't feel the sadness, the loss or pain
I feel constant anger at myself and a false happiness
But I don't know why it feels false
I really am happy, but without the sorrow it doesn't feel real
I see and hear so many reasons to be sad but it just
Flies over my head like paper in the wind
I don't want to hurt myself
Just feel something that will make the happiness seem real

YOU'D NEVER KNOW

If you looked at me, and not know my past
You'd never guess what I've been through
If I told you I've been depressed so bad I tried to kill myself and salf-harm
You'd never believe me
If I told you the first 12 years of my life were hell
You'd wonder why I'm no grateful and happy
If I said I hurt people when I am *really* angry
You'd laugh and think I was lying
If I told you my story
You might run away and hate me 'cause my past is so messed up
If you met my family
You'd judge me 'cause it's messed up, confusing, and guarded

FATE

We feel the pain
Hear the disdain
It's a fate you can't rewrite
You can't go back
Can't change the past
You're stuck with your past present wrongs
We can't escape

LIFE

Livin' in a world where it's all on fire
Gonna go to a place so I can take it higher
Never gonna give up, never gonna let it in
I'm always gonna fight, always gonna find my way
Always gonna be there when you say
Life isn't what it used to be
Life isn't what you thought it could be
It's changed, it's different, all rearranged
Your changin' and I know you can make it
If you keep your head held high and your eyes to the sky
We'll never know why we suffered our pain
Never know why people hate who we've become
It's all in the works of the world

MUSIC

I feel the beat beneath my feet
I hear the song in my ears
I have a wish on my mind
I need love to run through my heart

RUN

Let's run away and live forever
Try and forget our long past
Let's go and be together
Try and be always at last
Let's join hands and say it
Try and be here forever
Let's get together and never end it
Try and never say never

LOVE

Love means you never give up or quit
It means you push on no matter what
Love means you try your hardest to make it work
It means you stay by their side until they die
Loves means you always tell them the truth
It means you say you love them
Love means you comfort them when they cry
It means you help them up when they fall

FIGHT

I won't ask for you to help me fight my battles
Physical or mental
But that doesn't mean I don't need you
If you come and help me fight
No matter what I do
I'll always love and care about you

GO

If you want to leave
you can
I won't stop you
If I don't mean anything to you
Go your own way
You don't have to care about it hurting me
'Cause I'm already hurt
Don't worry about my broken heart
It was broken long before your time
But don't stay 'cause you feel you have to
Then you'd be lying to me

TEARS

A tear falls from her eye
Rolling down the face, it falls to the floor
The heart was broken and beaten again
She hides her pain in secret smiles
The cuts are masked behind her sleeve
Her bruises are hidden behind her clothes
She keeps her tiny shred of hope
Hidden away safely
But she'll never forget her tears

NEVER

I never knew my walls would fall
Never knew someone could penetrate my resistance
I never thought they could melt my fears
Never thought I'd fall without truly falling
I never knew someone could get my trust right away
Never knew they'd care this much
I never thought I wouldn't be guarded enough
Never thought my heart would heal
I never knew someone could make me whole
Never knew I could feel complete again

YOU'LL NEVER KNOW

You'll never know my secrets
I hide them too well
You'll never hear my story
I can't speak it
You'll never see my tears
I just wipe them away
You'll never feel my fear
I tend to block out that pain
You'll never know how I cope
I keep it to myself
You'll never hear my pleas
I shut up a long time ago
You'll never see me smile a true smile
I tend to fake them all
You'll never feel my weakness
I hide that from the world
You'll never know, oh never

DO YOU?

Do you understand what fear is like?
Do you know what we've been through?
Do you know what a burning hell feels like?
Have you witnessed the worst things imaginable?
Have you cried out in fear but never been heard?
Have you hid the marks from everyone?
Have you faked the smile that you wear?
Do you know what pain feels like?
Do you understand how I see the world?
Do you know my fear?
Do you know what we've seen?
Do you know what we've heard?
Can you comprehend our tears?
Can you hold us and never feel our fear?
Can you tell us it'll all be ok?
Can you look into our faces and act like you don't know?
Do you really understand us?
Do you look at us and see our pain?
Can you say you know us?
Can you say you have it right?
Can you judge us because of what we wear?

Can you say we're weak?
Can you look into our faces and laugh?
Can you mock us because you don't understand?
Do you understand how we feel?
Do you?
Can you?
Have you?

BROKEN

The dark is closing in
The pain is taking over
I can see the blood on my soul
I can feel the denial in my heart
I know I'm falling
I know I'm dying
I see the things I've never seen
I see the tears rolling down my cheeks
I try to push it out
I try to have no doubt
I say I care
I say I can make it
You see my smile
You see me fake
I hide my tears
I hide my fears
I'm broken
I'm never going to be fixed
This isn't something I can control
This isn't the monster you want to know
I can't let you be
I can't let you see

I'll hide it till I die
I'll live it till I cry
You'll never love me
You'll never care
I know you're faking
I know you're making
You can't hide this from me
You can't take away the lie
I'm broken
I've bled
I know this pain is never ending
I know the sorrow will be mending

YOU NEED TO KNOW

I'm writing this to tell you
That I'm beyond repair
You think that I am perfect
But I know you don't know
So here it goes
I've lived in a burning hell
And now I'm burning
I've been beat so bad
My heart's broken down
I cried to the sky
I never let them see
I know you think you can fix me
But I'm beyond repair
I know this is true
I shouldn't even bother
To try and love you
One day you'll be gone
I'll be left to pick up what you dropped
You say you care
And I want to believe you
But how do I know

That you don't fear
My heart is broken
From my hell
I'm not safe
And you'll never know
'Cause when I try
I want to cry

QUESTIONS FOR YOU

Can you see me?
I'm in tears
Can you feel it?
I'm leaving
Can you tell?
I'm never coming back
Do you know why?
I'm falling
Do you know how?
You're right here
Do you get why?
'Cause I care
Will you follow?
'Cause I'm lost
Will you take my hand?
I'm scared to death
Will you stay with me?
I don't want to be alone
Is this something that you want?
I want it too

Is this something that you care about?
I hope you do
Is this something you'll always love?
I love this too.

MY HEART

It's falling to the ground
See it? That's another piece
Do you know what that is?
It's my heart
Yet again it's broken
I know you don't get it
So I'm going to break it down
That's my fear, all my doubt
That's the thing that people hate
It's the piece people let break
You think you know why
I'll let you know
It's you, it's me, it's them
Do you get it now? No?
You are letting me fall
And I know it will kill me
I'm not stopping this
And it's getting scary
They are all behind us
And I'm alone
I know you can't fix this
So you can just go

You don't need what I'll bring you
You don't need my fear
I'll just bring you down
I know you'll leave me here
It's not like I don't care
It's not like I don't want you
It's that I do care and don't want to hurt you
It's that I do want you and it'll kill me
I'm dying, don't try and stop it
I'm breaking, don't try and fix it

TRIED TO LET IT GO

I tried to say it
Tried to mean it
Tried to let it go
I tried to end it
Tried to beat it
Tried to let it go
I tried to see it
Tried to hear it
Tried to let it go

LOOKING

I saw her and so did you
Looking for answers to unasked questions
I saw him and you did too
Looking for reasons where none can be found
She saw me and so did he
Looking for love in the most hateful way
She saw me and he did too
Looking like the devil hiding in the dark
I'm looking while she is too

Just one touch and I'll turn you to dust. Blown away by the wind and gone like rust

We didn't get here by luck. We got here through faith, strength, hope, and forgiveness. We loved, not hated. All those blood, sweat, and tears wrote their own stories.

A beauty untold is a beauty unknown and a beauty unknown is a beauty unchanged.

Let's go back to blowing dandelions and wish on a wishing star. Let's go back to when a weed and flower couldn't be told apart. When one word could open up a door to a whole new world. Let's go back to when our innocence was our most treasured gift.

It's not as simple as who I am or what I've done
It's about how long I've lived and what I know
My life has never been simple
The world has never cared for me
All my scars, abandoned and rejected
All my wounds, beat and cut
Each cold voice, taking me down
Each cold whisper, freezing my soul
Take my hand, it won't be safe
Take my heart, please thaw it

A fist raised, to fly through the air
Cries in the night, with no one there
Words thrown up to be caught by you
Breaking, you're torn in two
Yet, here we are again
Fighting me is careless, this just began
I'm the only one committing the crime
All that's happening is you're lost in time

To fight for my life,
To run from strife.
I know I'm about to die.
To tell the story.
To give up glory.
I know you'll fail to understand
I reach out with broken faith
I feel like I'm losing space
Gasping for air in a place not so near
How do I live?
How do I give?
To the unknown fate that awaits me

The tears I cry on nights while I fly. Taking my pain and sin far away. Unknown in the distance, but seen in the light, are the eyes I hide. Bring me closer to the fear inside, a raging monster ready to fight. The tears no one sees, breaking a heart whose soul is all but several years old. The fragile skin, the protection of light, and a faith I've never seen, saved me.

He's the pain I feel inside
A heart that's breaking each side
Our story is tragic, filled with pain
No matter what, I'm still insane
A monster given the fire
It's burning me and all this attire
Never will we rise to see a band new day
There's nothing left for anyone to say

Death, yet once my friend, still betrayed me
With his silky robes, of darkness black
He whispered in my ear my time that only I have left
As his hand, he outstretched, I held onto the soft palm

You don't understand my hopes aren't high
I spill the poison, show my blood
A mark on my skin, a painful memory
As I try to get my wish
Each last moment only I can't have
See, I've tried two times over
Spilled a secret, one
Asked and questioned love, two
No idea, lack of clues

Where the monster hides
The devil takes its dwelling
Inside this young mind
Only dark is swelling
Blood of uncut veins
Flowing to the ground
Cries in the night
Hearing that loud sound
Words spoken
Less and less
A beautiful life
What a mess
Will I live
To see the light?
No dear, I think not
Only just night

THE END

A frozen soul broken at a once new whole
Tired and fragile as I once was
An infant I cry for a lost love
Cries in the night, always ignored from life
This blood shows I'm still alive
While she hangs from a fixture like a puppet
Praying for a second chance
Waiting in the dark with an unlit candle
Quiet, here comes the devil
You can't hide from those demons inside
Run as fast as you can
This is the end

ONE MINUS ONE

The walk she takes, slowly unravels
Truth only spoken in her dreams
Works spoken one minus one
Hallways always haunted with ghosts
Whispers follow every step
Stories she never knew are told
Marks on her skin from a dangerous rage
Slices and slivers for a terrible pain
Words spoken one minus one
Tempted to hang from the loving rafters
A beautiful necklace to take some pain away
That's all she has left... or maybe ever had
Those demons waiting in the dark
Take that blade, make that cut, spill that blood
Make it long, from palm to elbow
Dress up nice, put on that necklace
Fly with the rafters
Words spoken one minus one
One less "hi", one less laugh
Now she's gone

AGAIN

One simple request
Not innocent, not fair
To raise a hand
I touched a soul
Bleeding, I knew
Yet again I broke you
Grasp at the straws
Gasp for a last breath
Shake me awake
From this dark terrible nightmare
Your eyes, my dear
Why so many of those fears?
Shed me a tear for a hopeful luck
Help, you cry
Tell me about your dead end life
This bruise, that cut
My hands are raised
You pain is my life
It's the only way I can survive
A shadow over me
As I shadow over you
A touch so cold

I shiver in pain
Like glass I break
A fire melts away my disguise
You know me now
I can't run away
Why are you in so much pain
A sharp pain, stabbing your side
Crack against your skull
That pain in your eyes, in your walk
From me I know
Delivered from the devil on my shoulder
Shuddering, it's freezing now
I'm sorry, you have to die again inside

LIGHT OF LOVE

The touch of love
Wraps around the soul
It chokes out the darkness
And infects you with light
Slowly, close you pull in
'Till you're sharing each breath
Moving in a dance
To music of each beat
Holding it close
So you never let it go
Keeping it in your arms
Letting the light flow
Sharing each word
All but those three
Letting the meaning roll off the tongue
Filling in the empty spaces
Releasing the beauty of the soul
And coloring the heart
Falling at a rate
Where slowing isn't possible

Fear that's always seeping in
Slowly bleeding it all dry
Sucking out your love
And filling it with hate
Breathing each last breath
Till you have no more life
Welcoming the death
Of a love you knew as true
Trying to close the walls again
But struggling with it no more
Closing off the light
Hoping it'll fade away
Them pulling you in
Until drowning is all you know
They're holding you
Trapping you in a love you fear
Delicately believing in them
While keeping in the fear
Trying to love them
In a darkened past
Running the race
With death following
It's catching up
Until they hold your hand
They're pulling you along
Even though you're still falling

Keeping you alive
With each breath you share
Finally, the end it near
It's right behind with the line right there
Taking the last steps
To a final win

ADDICTION

The poison seeping through your blood
A high to last for just moments
Dead soon will be who you are
Heart beats slower and slower
As you are dying, hoping its not real
Won't no one be there to save you
Falling and begging on your knees
You fail yet again to understand
It's a monster tearing out your soul
Fight all you want because you won't win
Success is a losing game for you
Try with all you have to be the top
Bones breaking with each motion
No, god can't help you now
In the devil's hands you go
Run all you want because you can't move
An anger fuels your mind until you're done
Tell me, was this part of the plan
Did you want to crumble
You break under all the weight
Are you dead yet, shame
Talk about that burning pain

Screaming till you lose your breath
This is your moment, don't forget
You can leave with a terrible ending
It's you story, it's your end
Goodbye my dear
You're finally in the end's doom
It's done, your gone at last

MONSTER

She's not a game, don't test her strength
It's like deadly poison
Seeping through my veins
Soon, it's not mind, body, or soul in my control
I seem to be in the dark
Under a spell
Fighting to be freed of this
She's not a toy, don't release her for fun
Hiding in the darkest places
With one simple touch
She becomes what you fear
She's not me, she's *in* me
We seem like friends
Only to make me bleed
At the end
She comes with a fear
And leaves me in tears

DEATH

Closer you come to an eternal doom
A darkened soul to always consume
Stripped to a vulnerable fear
The depth to a golden heart we'll bear
Seeping red soaking an empty bowl
Overflowing into the icy cold
Gazing into an unending abyss
We're nothing it going to miss
Holding on with no way to cope
Soon to be a broken hope
Falling slowing without a grip
Failing to see where we'll soon trip
Hate filling every space
The knowing coming at an unknown pace
Changing each direction you go
Never listening to the answer no

ANGER RED

(Poem about Tybalt from Romeo and Juliet for English Assignment)

In this love, you are the end
Liquid red slain by the dark's night blue
Death by the hand of a family true
Thirst for revenge as a flower thirst for water
A boiling rage from a toxic waste to an unending monster feeding a feud's last once true to an unending embrace of an immortal anger
Blood seeping from life's last breath
Ripped is the shirt of 20 rich pieces
A wish to break this unending circle
Fire burning through the tiger's flesh
Love is hate as hate is love
The anger, like a sour taste, is a never ending cycle
The rotting smell of a pale body
Death seeps in like water seeps in cracks
The killer is told "run"
And the last breath of anger red slips away

LOVE TO DEATH

(Poem about Romeo from Romeo and Juliet for an English Assignment)

You stand there, soon to lie in your own doom
A dark turn gold then tarnished
Mending a heart with a huge scar
As gallant as a fox
Climbing the wall leading to an unknown future
setting the tale of inevitable love that bleeds into a
hate spreading through the soul, ending in death
This was always ended from the start
A blood stained shirt from your sin
You wish time would slow for love
Like a swan, she stands there
More to a love, then love to a hate
You, with a pride too strong, run away
Sweat dripping down a red face filling the nose
with a sour smell
As doomed as darkness is to light
Why, my love, why
You, a young man, goes from heartbreak, to love,
to death, goodbye.

TEAR IT APART

I hold in my doubt
Inside I shout
Those marks on my skin
They're scars of a darker sin
Don't say you see my pain
I'm almost insane
There's a monster inside
One that I try so hard to hide
I can't hear "it'll be okay"
All I want is not to stay
This anger is black
My mind goes so off track
Why is this so hard
Life hasn't given a single good card
That's my heart
Tear it apart

THAT'S WHEN YOU KNOW

When love is hate and hate is love
And pain is peace and peace is pain
When life is death and death is life
And wish is waste and waste is wish
That's when you know you're hurt
When the same is the opposite and the opposite is the same
And want is need and need is want
When white is black and black is white
And light is dark and dark is light
That's when you know you're alone
When try is do and do is try
And whole is broke and broke is whole
When left is right and right is left
And cut is sow and sow is cut
That's when you know you're hated
When hope is hopeless and hopeless is hope
And lost is found and found is lost
When you is I and I is you
And mad is glad and glad is mad
That's when you know you're unloved

When loud is quiet and quiet is loud
And hard is soft and soft is hard
When right is wrong and wrong is right
And tough is weak and weak is tough
That's when you know you're done

DEPRESSION

There's darkness in my head
It'll often creep in my bed
While I wrestle with it in my sheets
Please know, there aren't any cheats
All too many things to say
None of it will make your day
This darkness, it feeds on hate
One day, maybe you'll be too late
The darkness has a story
A story violent and a little gory
It was once my trusted friend
With a promise to stay until the very end
You see why the friendship was so toxic
Those conversations, always just one topic
But there was a catch when I broke it off
Breaking its promise made it scoff
As hard as I tried, it just wanted to stay
It made a promise, so of course it'd never stray
This is why there's a darkness inside
No matter how hard I try to hide
It's just like it said
It'll be there until I'm dead

THE HALLWAY

A hallway dark, cold, and dim
No light, no love, no hope
There it is, in the corner
A frozen soul, curled away
Close I step, rising my fear inside
A dress, blonde hair, rocking back and forth
Next to it is the cursed door
I've chained the devil's monster inside
I hear it, calling out a name, my name
It's calling, not for me, for it
A tear falls, I can hear it hit the ground
Screaming, I finally know
This hallway is haunted
Ghosts from a broken heart
There are too many doors
Turn back, there's no way out
Banging all I want, no sound I make
Forward is the only way to go
I feel the fear as I come close
Another tear, another call
Try so hard to run away
I hover over it, too scared to touch

A hand reached out, grabs me as I fall
Back in time to the beginning I go
I can't breathe as a man draws near
I scream, no sound comes out
Daddy? Momma?
Yelling, screaming, word after word
Block out the noise, impossible
Then there she goes, once again gone
I'm ripped through time once again
Pulled away, no more place to go
Again, I have no home
Time after time, night after night
Then, there he is, on top pulling at the strings
My eyes open to it's only reason
Through time again I flew
It's *her* again, I feel my hands sweat
Pounding in my ears
In death's hands I want to be
The screams of pain
Blood flowing from my open veins
I can taste the poison
I'm dying ever slowly
Suddenly I'm back in the hallway
It's head turns at a slow pace
Those blue eyes, I mirror them
That sigh is mine
A little girl, 6 or 5
My tears they flow

I fold her in my arms
You're finally safe my dear
I saw the story only she could see
And now her life, we can breathe

TAKE A PILL

The voices in my head
Whispering "you should be dead"
Crazy how they sound like her
My enemy who left no cure
I'll just take a pill
All so I can chill
There is an endless battle
A war, it's time to mount the saddle
It's chaos in my mind
Peace you are oh so hard to find
I'll just take a pill
All so I can chill
Therapy is hit or miss
Maybe I can't take a diss
Doctor said "sounds like anxiety"
But how, when it feels like I'm fighting a deity
I'll just take a pill
All so I can shill
I'm fighting a war that costs a major bill
So I'll just take a pill

THING CALLED ANXIETY

There is a chaos swirling
A storm could keeps on curling
The war that rages
And those things released from their cages
Can't you see me there, bruised and bleeding
Somehow my life is impeding
I just want to rip out my hair and cry
Because I know I cannot die
But this things says "you're better off dead"
And I keep screaming "get out of my fucking head"
Doctor said "sounds like anxiety"
But what do you mean, 'cause it feels like a goddamned deity
This monster inside of my brain
Sometimes I feel I'm fighting in vain
She said "take this pill"
But how they fuck does that pay my overdue bill
This thing says "give me your life"
"And if you don't give it, I'll cause you strife"

So you're saying those in that glass
Will pay off the debt and this will pass
'Cause this thing called anxiety
It just part of society

SAYING GOODBYE

This rose of red
That man lying in my bed
And a heart of gold
My, your heart feels old
It's a different feeling
My poor heart isn't healing
He told me he didn't love me
There is so much that will flee
What did I do wrong?
Should I have sang a different song
I think I always knew this ending
But parts of me hoped it wasn't pending
The love i have for this man
A future together was my plan
Now we will say goodbye
And a part of my heart will die

HIS OBSESSION

This dark soul has always been a "friend"
Holding me late at night until the very end
Always whispering his sweet poison in my ear
Until all I want is to disappear
But what you can't see
Is he isn't very good to me
He provided the blade
That I used to cut my skin I'm afraid
As I bled, he held me close
This is the toxic relationship I chose
He found me when I was low
I've always been told "you reap what you sow"
Can't you tell, he pulls all my strings
And the wounds, it always stings
This dark soul secretly was my foe
It's hard for me to let go
He came when I was broken and alone
Those dark intentions never shone
His name is depression
And somehow I became the object of his obsession

FIVE MONSTERS

There are monsters inside of my brain
5-to-1 I forever fight in vain
BPD, she's the king
Such a deadly song she can sing
Depression has lived here the longest
Feeding him made him the strongest
Next, anxiety thinks they're the big boss
When she's in control I'm often cross
Self-harm was the first child
Don't worry, compared to the last he's mild
Lastly there is suicide, his comments are often snide
This small family of monsters
Have become my trauma's sponsors
Flashbacks
Panic attacks
Are paying for the war
Until I am deadly sore
I wave my flag in surrender
These five and I will live in the fire's ember

FALSE GOOD-LUCK CHARM

Sometimes I miss it
The harsh kiss from each slit
False promise "I'll take your pain"
It's almost as addicting as cocaine
As I sit here with this blade
I think "with this my due are paid"
Dripping red, eccentric high
All from these cuts along my thigh
A 'coping skill', so dark and cold
Will the habit ever fold
The child of depression and anxiety
Along with the trauma from society
Living inside my brain forever
It's such a hard endeavor
While you call it self-harm
I call it my false good-luck charm

THE FINAL ADO

Its swirling through my mind
The emotions and words all too hard to find
That "sorry for all your pain and suffering"
Like some part of you was buffering
Did it really take you thinking you would die
For you to finally acknowledge your lie
When I had to heal without it
None of these broken pieces seem to fit
You got forgiveness you didn't deserve
All so I could cut the curve
You called me last week
But lord knows what you seek
A relationship between us
God I want to fucking cuss
Together we were toxic
It made everything so chaotic
The nerve you have to hope for shit
Just because dying made you want to admit
And now I cry for you, mourn for you
Because yet again I bid you a final ado

THE CLIFF'S EDGE

I feel like I'm on a cliff's edge
I've been here for years
Trying to decide whether to turn back
To jump, run, skip, or fly
Below me are sharp rocks
And rushing waters
Behind me is the hell escaped from
Fire and brimstone
I'm standing on unsteady ground
The land is breaking and crumbling
The wind is howling
Consuming my screams and cries for help
The hail and rain tumble down
Striking and bruising me without relenting
The thunder rumbles
Overtaking any other sounds
The lightning strikes
Illuminating the chaos around me
All the elements are against me
Hoping I'll fail
Hoping I'll give in
Hoping I'll break

Voices in the shout:
You are worthless
You have no purpose
You are a failure
You are alone
Nobody will care if you just give up
Nobody will care if you just give in
It's you time to die
I have been trying so hard
To survive
Because god I want to
Fucking thrive
If you look closely
You will see
This chaos is the result
Of a never ending war
A battle that has been raging
Since I first drew breath
So many demons out for blood
Out for *my* blood
I've waved my flag
A million times
To them
To you
To everyone
And it was always ignored
This will not stop
Until they have me dead

Despite my screams:
Get out of my fucking head
These cuts and bruises
Broken bones and scars
Tell the story
Of a war torn country
Despite all of this
A small light shines
I'm truly unsure where it came from
Let alone who sent it
It just suddenly appeared
Next to me
Holding my hand
And protecting me
Though the elements can still reach me
The light gives me
Warmth
Strength
Courage
And hope to stand on my feet
The only thing
It said was:
"Do not die on your knees
Let alone live there"
As it helped me up
It continued by saying
"Acknowledge the pain
It is ok to embrace it

Comfort and care for it
The pain will not fade
If you continue to let it bleed
Let people in
Let them shelter you
From the elements
You do not need to fight on your own
You have warriors at your disposal
Ready to take up arms to supper you
It is ok to scream and cry
But only in defiance
Not surrender
You must never surrender!"
When I asked:
"Where have you been all this time?"
The light smiled sadly:
"I have always been here
However you would not open your eyes
Or accept me
So I remained hidden deep in your soul
I have heard all your cries
And it killed me to know
You refused to let me help you
But I am here now
I will guide you
But be warned
I can help you through this war
I can give you strength

But you must continue to fight
With me, with us"
Around us
The chaos continued
But now I could see
The beauty in
The war
And the storm
For once
It did not seem
So all consuming
For once,
Faith stood
Hand in hand with me

YOU AND I

The blood will boil
My plans you will not foil
Pain is on the rise
I am something you cannot surmise
Even in the darkest night
Despite those who give a hard fight
This is a battle of will
I will not rest until I kill
Try oh try all you want
I will continue on like a taunt
I lay with you late at night in your bed
I scream endlessly in your head
Just so you know I want you dead
It'll all be over when I cut your thread
Come on, use your might
Pretend you don't feel fright
Challenge me I dare you
Just as I thought, it isn't something you'll do
Stand on the edge
Shh, it's ok to jump the ledge
screaming, scratching, clawing
I'm the thing in your stomach gnawing

You will ask my name
But dear, it's never the same
Have you yet gone insane
No, I don't want to hear you complain
I'm your never-ending king
Forever suffering with this song I sing
We are connected, you and I
Until the very day we die.

'TILL DEATH DO US PART

The church bells ring
And the choirs sing
Slow walk down the aisle
My "happiest day" is a deadly trial
When I get to the altar
He takes my hand without falter
Preacher says with a start
"Do you take her 'till death do you part"
His dark smile my only clue
He whispers "I do"
Preacher looked to me
There is no way out I see
"I do" with silent tears
All this confirmed my fears
He vows to have and to hold
Until the day I die old
Forever better and always worse
I knew he was a curse
I vowed to let him in
Allowing him to always win
Until the day I die

God I want to fucking cry
Preacher did not cease
"Speak now or forever hold your peace"
I looked to the immense crowd
No one said a single sound
Preacher spoke light as a feather
"You are forever together
'Till death do you part
This ring binds you to one heart"
It was then that it happened
My demon's kiss was blackened
In that moment I knew
Death was the only way through.

PAST, PRESENT, FUTURE

Not that long ago
I once had a conversation
With the three versions of me
My past self was bruised and bleeding
You could tell she was barely hanging on
Life had kicked her down a trillion times
And there was no end in sight
Honestly, she was so pitiful
My future self stood tall and proud
She dressed beautifully
And held herself with elegance
There was confidence in every step, every word
But she also gave off an air of comfort
And there was kindness in her smile
And I was somewhere in between
I gave off happiness and healing
My smile was neither broken nor big
And my heart held hope
I turned to the past
With tears in my eyes
"I'm sorry" I spoke

"I shouldn't have been so hard on you;
Forgiven you and given you a break;
I never should have cut into your skin;
And I never should have bled your soul.
I should have been protected
And I should have fought back harder
I am so truly sorry
For all I have put you through"
Past looked at me
Anger in their eyes
"I hate you
Not for all you've done
But for how you've overcome
How can you have hope?
How can you start to heal?
When all you've known is pain and suffering!"
All I could do was cry
Until future stepped forward
She embraced me in a way that made me safe
She wiped my tears
Brushed my hair from my face
Then held her hand out
For past to take
"My dears, please stop your fears
I have known you both
Longer than you've known yourselves
No matter how dark the moment,
No matter how broken and shattered

You will always stand as tall as you can
Whether on your knees
Or on your feet
You fight with every breath you take
I am sorry for your hurt
I am sorry fo the anger
But these things will not last
Hold tight to faith
And you'll walk towards the light"
In our tearful goodbyes
We knew we'd be ok
Because together
We had always been ok

There is a darkness inside
A voice in my head
No matter how I try to hide
This thing forever wants me dead
Supposedly, she's my friend
She's always been with me
And will be 'till the very end
I'm trying to escape, can't you see?
For so long, an unnamed monster
I tried so hard to lock the cage
But she tricked me like an imposter
And now I suffer her endless rage
Shh, quiet my child
Don't fight, don't scream
I'm really just mild
I want us to be a team
She's the voice that whispers
"They do not love you"
She's all those voices, so disperse
"Why did you let them walk away?"
Telling me "you are worthless"
I'm screaming, clawing

"You have no purpose"
It's this thing that's gnawing
"Fuck it, go fuck him"
I now live with this disease
All from my sin
I just keep begging "stop please"
"You should die"
I want it to go away
"I'm not telling a lie"
I'm the one it will slay

DEAR MENTAL ILLNESS

Hello, my name is... you know what, no, because you already know it don't you? You've known me most of my life, hiding in the darkest corners, creeping around on tip-toes. Coming into the light long enough to cause utter chaos in my life, breaking me, and beating me down, just to retreat and leave me to clean up *your* mess. Because of you, I have been shattered in pieces, bleeding onto everyone I love. You are the poison in my blood, the voices in my head, the pain in every orifice of my body, every cut against my skin, and every suicide attempt. You whisper lies in my ear, telling me things my heart tries desperately to fight. But somehow you always win, you always break my heart, and take a piece with you every time like I'm some hide and seek game. You get off on my pain, my suffering, my bleeding, and my shattered heart and soul. It fuels you. It helps you grow, and the more I fight, the bigger you get it seems. You hold my head underwater, so I'm struggling to breathe while I'm drowning.

But guess what? I'm in control now, not you. I'm growing while you shrink. I am the one that will win this war, not you. I am strong, not you. I am the survivor, neigh the fucking thriver. How dare you take over my life? How dare you break me? How dare you control me? How dare you tell me I am worthless? How dare you tell me I'm not loved? How dare you tell me I have no purpose? How fucking dare you?! Watch me defy you, watch me overcome you. Wave your flag now beauce I fight to win. I will *never* surrender, *never* back down. Whether on my feet or on my knees, I raise my sword to fight with ease. You can't break me. You can't touch me. You can't poison my mind, body, and soul anymore. You can't lie to me. And you can't fucking hide from me. So bring it on, you'll see who wins

Sincerely,
A warrior

THE JOURNEY

The darkness is swirling
Utter chaos is curling
Voice are screaming
It feels like I'm dreaming
This monster is all consuming
It'll be here forever, I'm presuming
There's a bridge coming
The cold wind is numbing
Everything around me is crumbling
And, oh lord, I keep fumbling
If I cross to the other side
There awaits my guide
His robes are black
Over his shoulders is a pack
Inside are all his tools
To help me conquer my ghouls
Am I going to survive
Nothing wants me to thrive
I want to cry

Everything wants me to give up or die
But fuck no
I'll never stoop that low
This journey has been so different
But the goal will be so magnificent.

CONQUERED

There is a war that rages
I've locked many monsters in cages
Waving my white flag
All while sick with the plague
Toxic chemicals filling the air
I'm not one they will spare
Counting every single second
It's a win I can't beckon
Blood soaked swords
Demons come in hoards
Those days are numbered
I will not be conquered
Each breath I take
This is all so hard to fake
My warriors stood strong
They've been by my side all along
We've shed blood, sweat, tears,
Just trying to overcome our fears
The hounds are out
They'll find us, no doubt

On and on I'll fight
Long into the darkest night
Their days are numbered
We will not be conquered

HOLD MY HEART

The touch of love as light as a feather
Always there, despite the weather
Through any hard or easy endeavor
You'll hold my heart forever
The feeling of love as hopeful as the sun
I've never felt this for anyone
You're as handsome as ever
And you'll hold my heart forever
The time with love is patient
The feelings we have are aberrant
These tie they cannot sever
Because you'll hold my heart forever

MEANT TO BE

As I stood there, wind whipping my hair
You appeared to me, as thought thin air
On the dawn after my darkest nights
As I had barely won the fights
My faith in love was gone
And of all the cards I thought I'd drawn
Yours was my very last one
Hidden away at the end until I had none
With the first message
You took me in all that was my image
Held close, my heart I protected
I was forever dejected
Hand in hand with misery
My life was a parental advisory
I've fought so hard for love
In the end I couldn't rise above
But you came closer than close
Never any need for anything grandiose
Oh my love, you're one of a kind

I found you when the stars aligned
You mean the universe to me
And the angels above must have to agree
You and I are meant to be

PRESSURE

It's rock solid, my facade
"Blessed my God"
You'll never see the break beneath the surface
It feels like I'm drowning, I won't resurface
There's an all consuming refresher
I cannot fathom what they expect of me
Can't they just let me be?
Because I'll never let them see below
They can't know I feel so low
I'm trying to breathe
While I forever seethe
Grasping hard, holding fast
The final string might break at last
This pressure is growing stronger
And this break is getting longer
I long for just one moment
But this request seems so abhorrent.

ETERNAL SLUMBER

I feel so tired
But one more "you're late" and I'm fired
I just want to sleep
But my mental health I have to keep
There's so much going on inside my head
So please just let me go to bed
Will you be here to save me,
Or are you going to just let me be?
Tell me, am I worth it,
Or am I just a piece of shit?
I just want one time
Where rest is not a crime
And I won't die with the chime

THE FINAL BATTLE

A war that rages
She stands, defends the cages
Guilt, shame, and anger
Somehow became her anchor
She'll fight to the death
Soon she'll draw a final breath
Resilience and determination take the lead
Planting the truth, a seed
Blooming in the darkest night
Not quite strong enough to show it's might
Shh, lay down your sword
I'm here to cut the cord
They spread lies and fear
Please don't shed a single tear
She still won't let it fall
Her guard stands tall
Fighting on without relenting
She's learned only resenting
The flower blooms
Somehow clearing up the fumes
A small crack
All she has left is a final attack

Determination tries for peace
While resilience goes to speak
You've fought long
You've fought strong
Keep your faith
We don't want to take your space.
You no longer have to fight
I know you're drained of all but sight
Look around
This doesn't need to be a battle ground
We've done our protecting
It's no longer time for deflecting.
She dropped her shield
Onto the blood, sweat stained field
Her armor fell
And with that, it broke the spell.

www.ingramcontent.com/pod-product-compliance
Lightning Source LLC
Chambersburg PA
CBHW060453080526
44584CB00015B/1424